More Me
THAN I USED TO BE

— A —

Journey to Freedom

More Me
THAN I USED TO BE

A Journey to Freedom

Poetry and Photography by

MARIE SLIDER HENRIKSEN

Sliderbabe

For information contact:
marie@sliderbabe.com

Published by:
Sliderbabe Publishing

Content Editor – Debbie Ihler Rasmussen
authordebbieihlerrasmussen.com

Cover and interior book design by
Francine Platt • Eden Graphics, Inc. • edengraphics.net
Cover photo by Author

Paperback Black & White ISBN 979-8-89454-052-8
Paperback Color ISBN 979-8-89454-073-3
eBook ISBN 979-8-89454-053-5
Audiobook ISBN 979-8-89454-054-2

Library of Congress Control Number: 2025909201

Manufactured in the United States of America
First Edition

Dedicated to my Squad of Angels, on both sides on the veil;

I have never walked this journey alone.

TABLE OF CONTENTS

PREFACE

Sometimes I feel frozen. I can't speak what I am thinking or write what I am feeling; censoring myself based on what others may think. I worry I'll be judged or disliked by the majority, for my words. Then I remember to push through that fear and start speaking from my heart. This message may help just one person, and that is who I write for; the one who needs it now. That one person is you or the child sitting alone in their room, hearing their parents argue, and feeling like there is no hope in the world. It could be the man, who just lost his wife from cancer, and is looking online one last time before he chooses to join her. Or possibly, it's the alcoholic or addict, who just came to, in a pile of their own vomit, and feels like no one understands what they are going through.

I write for the minority. One day I hope they will be the majority with a new norm of finding peace by fighting to get to a better place, gaining empathy, love, faith and genuinely trying to appreciate each day they are given. This message is for the individual; each going through their own journey, who may need hope right now. They have known what it was like to be down with nothing except misery and contempt; lost in pain, controlled by fear, anxiety and depression. They have imagined the world without them and know what it's like to white knuckle through the night, wishing to escape reality, knowing the damage that would cause, so instead, pray in earnest to make it to morning, rocking and crying themselves to sleep. They know what it is like to grab, reach, and crawl through despair, or agony; barely making it on the other side to find love, empathy, and compassion from others who have already made it through on their journey. They have experienced how hard it was to reach for that helping hand.

I hope I will never be ashamed to share my story. God has shown me that it has helped others find him. By sharing the light, He continues building my strength to fight another day. I know at the end of the journey, there will be complete peace and serenity. For now, I will continue to write and speak. God will direct my words to the individual who needs to hear them today. To anyone else struggling like I have, with writing for an individual, instead of the majority opinion, I say, just write. Your thoughts, feelings, and entire existence is meant to be part of a bigger story, that we will one day see, and you are meant to connect with individuals. Forget those who try to tear you down or who are envious and irritated. God may use your words to save a life today, and tomorrow, they may save the life of the individual who tried to tear you down today. With God in your heart, just write.

THE JOURNEY 12/24/2017

A scared little girl was running to and fro,

Trying to find something, or someone, she didn't know.

A thousand thoughts were whirling and creeping inside her mind;

A doorway to her heart, in darkness, she couldn't find.

Then a fire started stirring and shining from up above;

A little spark of hope, of healing, and of love.

It started to brighten the gloomy way,

The path began switching from night to day.

As her feet began to twitch and tingle,

Her frame of mind went surely single.

She knew at that moment what she must do,

But where would she get the strength to make it through?

Ahead lay mush and cracks and stones,

That she felt would surely break her bones.

Bravely she began pushing, jumping, and moving,

Her heart muscles started slowly improving.

For as long as she kept her eyes,

On her next step toward her prize;

The path grew rails of hope,

And from the ceiling came a rope.

The gift of these tools helped her to fight,
In doing what she knew to be right.
And when she stood firmly at the door,
She had no idea what was in store.
But she knew that she need not show fear,
For suddenly a small peephole did appear.
When she began viewing what was inside,
She was truly filled with a humbled pride.
For her faith and good works were finally rewarded,
And the doubt inside her mind was completely aborted.
She knew in that moment she could never explain,
The unique peace that filled her heart, all words seemed too plain.
While faithfully pushing the door ajar,
She heard a soft voice 'boom' from afar;
"You're welcome here, I've missed you so!
But if you want, you are free to go,
And when you decide you want to return,
That negativity inside you, I'll gladly burn.
I've done it many times before,
But it's something you've forgotten or tried to ignore.
The love you are feeling can forever be yours,
This comfort is for all believers who walk through My doors.
When you finally decide to stay here with Me,
I promise I will carry you into Eternity.

FIGHT FOR FREEDOM 4/17/2018

At the end of the path the darkness gets thick,
I push my way through, feeling this is a trick.
When I finally see that door so inviting,
I feel my breath catch and I know I'm surviving.
Suddenly fingers start wrapping around me.
They pull me so hard; I fall to my knee.
They tug at my heart and tighten the strings;
They make me feel many negative things.
They get into my mind and wriggle my brain,
Changing my thoughts to make me insane.
They squeeze at my throat, my words disappear,
Until the end of my voice starts getting near.
They blindfold my eyes with a blur so intense,
The hope I saw before looks surrounded by fence.
They tie up my feet so I can't take a step,
Stealing away my vigor and pep.
They reach for my hands so I can't touch the knob,
My fingers I'm stretching, go numb and throb.
However, this journey that God sent me on,
Has given me muscles to help make me strong.
I pull out my hands from those fingers so tough,
When I finally realize I have had enough.
I wrench them off from strangling my voice,
Remembering through this, I always have a choice.

I whisper the words, faith in God does remain,
I ask for some help to escape this pain.
My eyes start to flicker, my sight is reborn,
I see the fingers now, and where my skin they have torn.
Behind me I feel a presence like ice,
Trying to intimidate, those eyes they do slice.
They feel like daggers all over my back,
And I keep reaching forward giving no slack.
Knob in hand I feel like a rubber band,
If I let go, in darkness I'll land.
I turn it as fast as I possibly can,
Feeling the cold behind like a huge roaring fan.
I pull open the door and His warmness engulfs me,
A feeling more grand than I could foresee.
His light from inside blasts out all around.
The fingers retreat; I am no longer bound.
My first step in Freedom, I gratefully take.
From the nightmare that was; I finally wake.

TRAVELING AGAIN 5/11/2022

I'm on that rough path again, though this time I see the lies,

That Satan often tells me, but God, he hears my cries.

Those rocks and sticks I've overcome, I thought would break my bones,

Have only made me stronger, many times I have been shown.

I'm not that same lost girl, who was stuck in the dark,

The warmth of that calm spirit resides within my heart.

The darkness tries to overcome, but this journey has let me see,

That I've walked this path before, and God can set me free.

I have to push myself again, to walk this path of sorrow,

And I know that, yet again, I may walk it tomorrow.

Today, however, I can find that door that's so inviting,

And be embraced by Heavenly Father, (isn't that exciting?)

He will always give me peace, if I reach out my hand,

And I know that one day, I'll permanently take that stand.

But, if I have to turn around, and take another journey,

Through the hurt and anger, that so often plague me,

I can always make it through, the path that is so rough,

Because I've faced it many times, which has made me tough.

Now that I know the tools, that always help me fight,

I try to help others, find that door of light.

Our journeys may be different, but parallel they are.

If they continue fighting, then they will make it far.

One day our hurt will end, and we will find relief,

We just have to find a way, to hold to that belief.

CONTINUING IN FAITH 12/05/24

Have you ever wondered what it's like to feel safe?

Or how you can find comfort when life makes you chafe?

Have you ever heard that voice from deep inside,

That tells you that it's time to get off this bumpy ride?

Have you been so lost, the idea of light was crazy,

And sitting in the darkness made you feel less hazy?

This is what my life was like, before the journey started,

And here is what my mind was like, before the clouds had parted:

"Unmet expectations,

resentments then frustration,

Then logic out the windows,

that's the way my brain goes.

Then loop-de-loop it goes around,

Solutions to this can't be found.

In it I can't stop this mess,

I'm going crazy I confess."

I couldn't find a path to safety, I felt I had to fight,

Everything and everyone, each day and each night.

I couldn't find safety, I didn't feel free,

Even though my life seemed so happy-go-lucky.

When I started on this journey, I found I wasn't alone,

Others had these same feelings; my mind was blown.

I didn't feel so isolated; they gave me tools to fight.

They showed me how they found God and came into the light.

When I started trusting Him, the One who is above,

He filled my heart completely with gratitude and love.

He started healing broken parts, with help from the Savior,

And really started changing the kinks in my behavior.

I have much to learn, and many layers to unfold,

I feel like a new story, in my life is being told.

I'm finding safety in the light, the darkness is retreating,

And in regard to others, I don't feel like I'm competing.

I'm continuing in faith, challenging that voice;

The one that tries to tell me, I'm making the wrong choice.

It tries to tell me I'm not worthy, or others are to blame,

And tries to overcome me with darkness and with shame.

Now that I have felt the warmth within the light,

It gives me strength as I continue in this fight.

I know all this is temporary, I have help to make it through,

Now I can turn my heart, to being there for you.

If you have felt the same as me, finding comfort in the dark,

I hope you get to read this and maybe feel a spark.

There is love around, that others can help you feel.

Sometimes, like me, you may have felt it wasn't real.

Please keep moving forward, the light will start to show,

From a loving God above who wants you all to know:

You have worth, just like me, even though our paths contrast,

And at the end of the journey, we will rewrite our past.

MORE ME THAN I USED TO BE

02/03/2018

All of my life I've collected pieces of varying sizes and shapes.

I don't know why I held some close and others I hid behind drapes.

Some people offered me distorted pieces and as a hoarder I couldn't see,

That even though they were part of a puzzle, they didn't belong to me.

They were part of someone else's picture, usually those who were trying,

To hand them over to me instead, of by their own box abiding.

Like them I too offered pieces, to others along my path,

And as I'm learning to step back, sometimes I have to laugh.

There are some holes inside that make the picture hard to see,

And other places I forced the shape of a distorted figure of me.

I know the image I manipulated, is not the one God made,

For He created everything beautiful just the way they were laid.

At some point I looked in other boxes wishing mine was different,

So I started mixing up our pieces creating "something magnificent."

I started forcing pieces together throwing others away,

Stealing some from other people and my picture changed every day.

Where I'm at now is trying to get back to the box that is mine alone,
And with the help of other people, God's will is being shown.
I'm learning how to pick up pieces, the ones I tried to hide,
By giving them to other people or thrown away in pride.
I'm letting go of the distorted ones that don't fit anywhere,
And giving them back to their owners, so their box won't be so bare.
God painted the picture on my box to be the way he desired,
And I'm done trying to change things, it makes me just too tired.
Slowly but surely as I get things in order, I know one day I'll find,
The picture that God had planned for me that got lost in my mind.
Pieces are finally fitting together; in the way I know He wants.
He's telling me that I'll be ok in my heart and in my thoughts.
The only thing I know for sure, is I'm more me than I used to be,
And I know the final piece of art is more perfect than eyes can see.

ACCOMPLISHING MUCH 01/07/2025

Moving forward in life and accomplishing much,

My potential in God has barely a touch.

The more I ask for, the more I receive;

He will not be limited by what I believe.

My past was messy, there was trauma and fear,

And I chose addictions, not God, to draw near.

Now I seek His guidance to heal from pain,

And ask Him questions; knowledge to attain.

I try to serve others, help them heal as well;

And show them how God broke through my shell.

If I get tired doing what God has asked,

His Son will carry me; His strength is vast.

God speaks His direction through the Spirit,

With a voice that echoes for the heart to hear it.

Sometimes I find that I need a break;

Yet He never scolds me like it's a mistake.

He simply says to get some rest;

After all, this life is just one big test.

It's not about shame and blame for myself,

Or even from others who watch from their shelf.

It's recognizing my struggles and strength,

Choosing to serve God, through any length.

Others who have chosen to serve,

Are sent to help me and ease my nerves.

Once rest has been found, eyes open to see,

Weak things are made strong unto me.

I move forward again following God,

Seeing pictures, inside, of a Heavenly nod.

I know as I'm productive and accomplish much,

I will be strengthened by the Savior's touch.

When this life is over, I can freely rest.

Knowing that I've done my best.

For with Christ's help, my mission will be completed;

In seeking God continually, I will have succeeded.

If along the way, I helped even one soul,

I know that, in Christ, I have made my goal.

INSANE SANITY 05/15/ 2018

This insane sanity that has taken over my mind,

Is something, I wish everyone could find.

It's the idea that in life, I can actually be free,

From doubt, shame, fear and misery.

For years I created many false stories,

Written in my own mind's laboratories.

Somehow, I knew, love couldn't be mine,

And pushing everyone away, was totally fine.

I told myself I would forever be,

Victim, burden, slave for eternity.

I told myself there was no way out,

Adhering to negativity and doubt.

I always had hope, one day things would change.

Yet I continued firing down that same lonely range.

I now know that was the true insanity,

Continuing on that path of righteous vanity.

My ego said I was better than everyone,

Because I was the only person who wanted to run.

When I finally let go, and let someone else drive,

My vessel stopped taking so many nosedives.

This is the thought that has taken over my life,

And cut through all the lies, like a burning knife.

The secret to escape from where I was caged,

Was learning my movements, were on myself gaged.

It took me a while to figure this out,

And I'm constantly learning to fight the bout.

When my brain starts to take control,

I ask God to shut it off, free my heart and soul.

In my mind there remains a daily fight,

I must ask Him again to let His will take flight.

I know if I depend on the One up above,

And those He put in my life, teaching me love,

My story may never actually shift,

Yet the clouds surrounding it will surely lift.

I'm a different storyteller than I was in days past,

And by reaching out, my insane sanity will always last.

MY SQUAD OF ANGELS 12/29/2017

They're not that far away; all those who passed before.

They're waiting for my arrival just behind this mortal door.

They're watching and guiding prayerfully in that space that's just beyond.

They're in the creases of my heart; a place they're very fond.

They're floating through my memories, to help sort out my past.

They want me to find happiness, but their flag is at half-mast.

They do this to help me bear the weight of struggles along the way.

They want to give their strength to me during every painful day.

They wait beyond my consciousness, their warmth they want to share;

Sometimes I feel it blowing in the wind that moves my hair.

I see them in a stranger's face as a flicker or a feeling.

Sometimes the similarities scare me through the ceiling.

I wonder if that person may be sent from one who passed,

Or if a chance connection is a hook my loved one's cast.

They're always looking out for dangers along my way,

Because a path of positivity may be just a choice away.

They speak to me with whispers heard with my heart not ears.

When I think of them with love, my grief slowly disappears.

When I start to change my thoughts from missing them with sorrow,

Into a beautiful memory, I get strength until tomorrow;

Then I start to feel them stronger, in the shadows that are cast,

And I know that our connection is NOT only in the past.

To me these thoughts do comfort and fill my heart with song,

For through my Earthly Journey, they will travel right along.

CONNECTIONS 03/12/2017

Sometimes I get this feeling, though sometimes it goes away,

I know that there are others, it shows in what they say.

I've been searching far and wide; a home to build so strong,

Where I can find comfort from this world that feels so wrong.

I'm learning I won't find it, if I hide my love and talents,

Playing the disconnect game, refusing to find balance.

When I focus on my past or future, forgetting the here and now,

Then I become a victim, worldly things may make me bow.

I start to judge another, "They are wrong and I am right,"

Or even worse, the feeling of giving up the fight.

In past I judged my worth on some opinions or advice,

Playing follow-the-leader in a swarming group of mice.

I pushed out the weaker being, stepping on their head,

Question is, what will I carry into my own death-bed?

I'll bring wisdom and emotions, with connections of the heart,

Not my worldly ambitions or even a piece of art.

There's so much to experience above my head and below my feet;

Many worlds to be discovered, many siblings yet to meet.

I sometimes get lost in arguing in my head or with another,

Forgetting that our perceptions are different from each other.

Even the yesterday me, I thought I knew so well,

Has changed so much today yet continues to still yell.

Sometimes I get distracted, about what to do or say,

Then I forget to focus on simple things that day.

There is a lot of healing, and amends that must be made,

I cannot stop experiencing the world as it's been laid.

That family of squirrels or bird's nest, I saw today around noon,

Did not come out of nowhere; it's been there many a moon!

A beautiful flower by the street, could have been easily passed,
He might have a brother where another shadow is cast!
The smile I saw on a stranger, I swear I've never seen before;
It might have graced my presence yesterday at the store.
I was just too focused on the things I had to buy;
Was he behind me with his kid, a teardrop in his eye?
The things that I've been blind to, may not be just by chance.
I may be missing some connections, a whole number left to dance.
A thin thread, like a spider's, is being shown each day.
I am learning how to follow it, in the vibe to do and say;
Not things that I have planned, ignoring how others feel,
But focusing on us both; watching layers start to peal.
I've experienced many things, some I cannot show or tell,
I have to give God credit, for helping me see so well;
That this invisible mighty strand is intertwining in my life,
And my energy or karma, impacts other's joy or strife.
I'm learning that my actions can certainly affect many,
If I serve another person, I'll be rewarded plenty.
It's not about the money, I don't need much of that,
It's not about the glory, or even the blessings I get back.
It's knowing that my words or even a helping hand,
May change split decisions, helping pearls transform from sand.
As I'm going through this constant changing healing,
I'm trying not to judge myself or focus on the feeling,
That I didn't accomplish everything I wanted to do today;
Because I know I did my best, if my motives didn't stray.
If by chance I realize I did some wrong somewhere,
I do my best to right it, or genuinely show I care.
I know if I stay positive, honoring connection to all,
The chains of negativity and pain will slowly start to fall.

MY TOOLS 05/01/2018

I was given two simple tools when I first opened my eyes.

They were both meant to help me, to get beyond the lies.

One was a ladder that extended way beyond my farthest sight;

One was a sturdy shovel to dig through pain or fight.

The goal was to move forward and share love along the way,

But somehow I got lost, and in pain I chose to stay.

Instead of using my shovel to help move the pain aside,

Or fight through the emotions, until they would subside,

I kept digging even deeper and the walls began to climb.

One day when I looked up I saw the cage inside my mind,

In that moment I remembered the infinite ladder on the edge,

And I hoped the extending power could reach down below the ledge.

In earnest I yelled out, hoping someone would hear,

And the One who gave the tools showed He was actually very near.

He threw me down the ladder, but again I got distracted.

I started digging yet again and the ladder never retracted.

Once I started noticing I was in pain and alone,

I looked up another time and could feel the sun that shone.

I cried out as I did before, thinking no one was listening,

But the ladder lowered down to me and I could hear Someone whistling.

Again I got lost in sorrow and grief, and kept digging my life away,

Until at last, I finally realized, that I was digging my very own grave.

I yelled and I screamed and then cried out loud;

I could not see beyond that stifling black cloud.

I blamed the One and Only, who had given me that shovel,

And anyone else's name, I could barely mumble.

Never once did I think I may be doing something wrong,

Until at last I cried out, "Can you please make me strong?"

This time with a thud, the ladder came crashing.

I realized in that moment what I'd been lacking.

For just the way I'd been working that shovel;

A ladder is meant to be climbed, not there to be groveled.

The One up above had been giving me chances,

A way to get out, but I only took glances.

I took a deep breath and with shovel in hand,

I grabbed onto that ladder, and lifted my foot from sand.

The roots of the hole like a strong jagged thorn,

Were the scars of my heart, trying to hook me to mourn.

They grabbed onto my clothes to be a distraction;

but I remembered that shovel was meant for protection.

So using that shovel, to break through the emotion,

I continued climbing upward, causing quite a commotion.

I must have looked crazy emerging from down below,

Swinging a shovel on a ladder; it was quite a show.

But as I looked around, tears filled my eyes.

I saw other holes around me and I could hear the cries.

You see I wasn't the only one who used the shovel the wrong way,

Most of us had gotten lost, and couldn't see the light of day.

There were other people, still, who were emerging from their holes,

As we interlocked our eyes, we finally remembered our lost goals.

With our shovels in our hands and our ladders leading the way,

We continued on our journeys, and knew we'd be okay.

UNDERSTANDING LOVE 02/05/2018

For years I knew the concept of love, though it took a very long time,

To understand God's plan for me, that love could really be mine.

Somewhere along the way my signals got all disturbed;

The idea of an actual love was absolutely absurd.

As my heart started reopening and the walls were falling apart,

The idea of true self-love is where I had to start.

My self-love began by learning that I truly am a daughter,

Given to faithful earthly parents to guide me back to Heavenly Father.

The next step was learning that God had given me a call,

So, I could escape the ramifications of Adam's original fall.

There is work that I am starting; filling my lamp up with oil,

And watering that seed of faith that was hidden beneath the soil.

I am starting to learn of charity, and humbling myself to Christ,

Although in my past I have denied him, more than only thrice.

God knew I needed help, to guide me along my way,

So, he sent me helping hands, to work with day by day.

He connected me with another brother, the Spirit who lives inside,

To help me buckle up, for ahead lay a bumpy ride.

He gave me sister Gaia, or Mother Nature as she's known,

To help keep me grounded, as the changing winds have blown.

I'm not sure what the future holds, or what awaits tomorrow;

However, I know I'm grateful for those testimonies I've borrowed.

I got them from others who've struggled and recognize God's hand,

So that I could have some kind of foundation I can firmly stand.

They've helped me find my missing peace, to soften up my heart.

They've helped me escape that lie inside, a new journey to impart.

The lie was that I didn't know love, and thought I had to run.

However, God has always shown it to me; He's loved me all along.

I just couldn't see, beyond the guilt and shame,

That I needed to fix my view and stop giving others blame.

I made choices in my past, that led me to dark places,

And as I look back now, I see the love in all those cases.

I was never alone, though I really did struggle,

Every time I asked for help, He pushed away the rubble.

So, to my family up in Heaven, and the ones down here below;

Whether I've met you before this day, or you're a sibling yet to know;

I promise I will try to love you, the way that God intended.

I know that while I'm doing this, my heart will be healed and mended.

I hope with my words and actions, others may one day see,

The love that God has for them, as others have shown me.

THE SEED OF HOPE 04/10/2019

A seed of hope was given, by one who came before;

I put it in my chest, to see if it could bore.

The roots began to dig so deep, they wrapped around my heart;

Planting themself firmly, so they could never part.

That hope grew strong as tree trunks, reaching to the sky,

Forever part of me, I'll have it when I die.

That seed of hope was planted, somewhere in my past,

And forever I will show the world, the way this hope can last.

Sometimes my hope it hibernates, and it seems pretty bare.

However I still feel it then and remember I must share.

My seed it must be watered first, but what can feed that hope?

I cannot rely fully on just the need to cope.

The want to share is great and all, for now work must be done.

For if I don't protect the growth, it could be overrun.

I must gain understanding, of how hope can be changed,

To faith where there's no room for doubt, that things have been arranged.

My heart it must be full of love, to give fluid to that seed,

And I must remember God's protection, I will surely need.

So, adding gratitude and smiles, overcoming doubt,

Helping those around me, releasing anger out;

Are things I do continually in order to sustain,

The power needed to grow out; the foundation to remain.

I stretch the branches from me, for others with empty hands.

The seedlings I share freely, if hope they can withstand.

The leaves that fall behind me, I know they will be followed,

By those who can't reach out, in darkness they have wallowed.

When they become ready, to draw eyes off the ground;

Patience, love and a seed, always will be found.

Some will not take the seed, others will throw it away,

But I know that if I tried today, today was a wonderful day.

CONFINED 02/22/2018

The simple thought to run, goes trailing through my mind,

At a million miles per hour, it almost makes me blind.

The idea that somehow I should have escaped;

The mental confusion, why do I feel raped?

That person never laid a finger on me.

The fear, nevertheless, was complete reality.

Feeling lost, torn, and broken, my nerves on edge,

I thought I'd lost these feelings, threw them off a ledge.

Yet a recent situation, made me feel confined,

My voice was left behind again, my body in a bind.

Though God protected me and let me walk away,

My heart is turned to others, who knew this pain today.

Those who felt like they were under attack;

Those who have no clue, how they can fight back.

Sometimes we are faced with people who are sick,

Or we get stuck in situations, we would never pick.

Sometimes things happen, no one likes to talk about,

And I see it's finally time, to let these feelings out.

For years I was lost from things beyond control.

It made me live in fear, darkened up my soul.

Instead of reaching out for help, from those I truly love,

Or even sending a prayer out to the One that lives above,

I made the choice to hide using anything in reach.

I gave poison to some people, and to others became a leach.

It took a Power greater than I could ever dream,

And a group of remarkable people, on whom I could lean,

For me to finally realize my worth was never gone.
I just had to figure out, my thinking was all wrong.
I had told myself that I was alone, no one could understand.
Then others stood around me and held me by the hand.
They had felt the same way, many years for some,
And they had found together, a reason not to run.
A Power even greater still, that no one can define;
He could take the pain away, completely from my mind.
When I finally humbled myself to ask for His wise words,
He blatantly told me to help other long lost birds.
He gave me a brand new voice, in writing He said I can heal,
Not just myself, to all who release the wheel.
I have to give voice to those who can't speak,
Because they are not ready, or feel they are too weak.
I have learned and I know, God will always listen,
And He sees my tears, the ones that glisten.
He knows my pain, and He wants all to know,
That His love is all around, even in shadow.
Sometimes we are blind, though His blessings abound,
And we need others to show us that love can be found.
That's what I needed to help clear my past,
And to learn that I needed to sacrifice the cast;
The one that I put on protecting my frail heart,
So I could finally address where I need to start.
Forgiving others and myself, is the answer to my freedom,
And I know that day is coming, it's finally the season.
With sharing my pain with others, I see the light inside.
It's starting to illuminate, and eliminate the pride.
I don't feel so alone, I know God will set me free,
And one day the pain will subside, for all eternity.

FROZEN 04/24/2022

Scared to heal, scared to live,
Why is there no care that I give?
Desire to run or walk away,
But can't take a step to get out of my way.
I'm frozen in a bubble of time,
Completely surrounded by dust and grime.
Cobwebs entangle my conscious mind,
Body entangled by ropes that bind.
Apathy threatens to take control,
Darkening my beautiful soul.
My light inside, it flickers and fades,
Isolation cuts like sharpened blades.
Fear of failure and fear of success,
My brain and heart are completely a mess.
Can't see a way out most of the days,
My mind's labyrinth firmly betrays.
Self-awareness, a strength to many who seek,
For a person like me, it just makes me weak.
The answers to questions are already found,
How to put them to work, is way too profound.
Feeling alone in this world of pain,
For many, relief is easy to attain.
Stuck in this loop day by day,
Consistently fighting to find a way,
To keep me from taking the easy way out,
Of running and hiding or lazing about.

Or going back to my old way of life,
Avoiding these feeling that cut like a knife.
Although these feeling are overwhelming,
The benefits of healing are very compelling.
The pain is a bridge to a new way of life,
I'm not sure what that is, while still in this strife.
But glimpses I've seen in the eyes of many,
The resemblance to God is completely uncanny.
Lots of work to be done, and patience to find,
To help me get out of the ropes that bind.
I've learned that I do not fight solo,

For help was promised a long time ago.
A Christ was born to take this pain,
So, happiness I can attain.
One day, I hope to understand this,
When He reaches out for my hand with His.
He will pull me up where I truly belong,
And I will praise Him in holy song.
To God, he will bring this humble girl,
The one inside me to be unfurled.
For she has been hiding under this mess;
She's been yelling out to me in distress.
I just keep on pushing her down,
But I know that to God, she will always be found.
God will embrace me with his heart,
And all of his love he will impart.
Then I will learn what this life really meant,
And understand why I chose to be sent.
With this reminder, faith again takes control,
Reminding me to keep God in my soul.
I can fight through these feeling, with help on my side,
And make it through this life's crazy ride.
Ancestors, friends, and family too,
Are there to help, my faith to renew.
Ups and downs will keep happening, that is a fact,
I have to keep fighting to get out of that act.
I keep telling myself to never give in,
For if I stay frozen, life will never begin.

NOT LOST 06/18/2020

Lost in my brain, feeling insane; not sure of where to go.

Yearn to be free; what's happening to me? In a boat I cannot row.

Thoughts reign supreme, or so it seems; where can I find release?

Where can I run? This is not very fun; why can I not find peace?

What's that I hear? It's not very clear; where is it coming from?

A pitter a patter, I feel like this matters; the noise is that of a drum.

It's not a loud sound, but it booms all around; a stirring within my heart.

The Spirit, it speaks; the brain starts to weep, for the curtains they finally part.

They show a love there, that the brain said was bare, and so I could not see,

How much I have grown; that I'm never alone; that Someone is holding me.

The scars that I've earned, are lessons I've learned and I cannot forget;

The fact of the matter; I did not shatter, and I will not live in regret.

So when I feel lost, and my brain feels tossed, I hope these words come easy;

"You can push through, this is not new, fear not I am with thee."

Fighting Pain and Despair

HAPPY DESTINY 09/18/2017

There's a road of hope for all to see;

It's the road to happy destiny.

And we must trudge through pain and fear,

To find the faith that gets us near.

But you can't get there with just faith and hope,

You must scrub your past as if with soap;

To conquer all your selfish ways;

To do what's right, just for today.

It's a road that anyone can walk,

And the directions are shared through friendly talk.

No one is forced to change their life,

They just choose to not live in painful strife.

They walk and talk the way they want,

But others are there when they need new thoughts.

They guide and help and teach and listen,

To be there for someone else, their only mission.

HOPE IN THE FIGHT 10/06/2018

The fight is still so real, it pulls me to and fro.

It makes me feel insane, like I have nowhere safe to go.

It yells inside my head, tells me I'm a fool;

That in seeking out some help, I'm just another mule.

I know that this is temporary, it will not last that long,

And the purpose of this fight, is to make me strong.

I know that there are others fighting right beside;

Yet part of me still wishes the fight would just subside.

Depression and anxiety fill me to the core.

I can tell you this much, this life is not a bore.

There's beauty still around, faith and love still there;

Even though I hide them, making me feel bare.

I won't give into evil, it cannot have my life;

Though it tries to overcome and cuts me like a knife.

I know that God is watching, offering His aid;

Sometimes it's through angels or offering a blockade.

Sometimes it's through man who offer a kind deed;

Or nature, music, scriptures; even in books I read.

I know He won't give up in helping me return,

There are just so many lessons I have yet to learn.

So, when I feel despair and my path seems hard to follow;

I look down at my feet and take one step towards tomorrow.

It's the only way I know that today I can bear,

The struggles set before me; and one day I can share,

The hope that kept me going on this journey I went through,

To the Glory in the end, when we are made anew.

A Change of Heart and Mind

THE POWER OF THOUGHTS
11/20/2017

Thoughts are more powerful than a thousand-pound weight.

They can push and pull inside you, change your focus from love to hate.

They can chain you down to the bed where you rest.

They can definitely guilt you for not being good, better, best.

They can contort the way all faces appear,

Especially the one looking back from the mirror.

They can make you assume the world would be best,

If you can just stop breathing with the rest.

They can make you see that darkness is better,

And there's no point at all to be a goal-setter.

Don't fret! The solution from all of this madness,

Is just changing those thoughts from pain to gladness.

You see, thoughts are more powerful than a million-pound weight.

They can lift you up higher than this mortal state.

They can open your eyes to a paradise of love,

Filled with a light as bright as the sun up above.

They can fill your heart with the connection we share,

With nature, each other, all things everywhere.

They can contort the pain in everyone's faces,

To become a gratitude of having been to those places.

They can remind us of old pains and fears,

So, we can be supportive and help others shed tears.

Again, thoughts are more powerful than anything you can imagine;

They actually control the heaven or hell you're living in.

So, I ask you today to go into your mind,

Alone or with help, go deeply to find,

The motivation to change your thoughts' point of view,

From pain, anger, sadness or anything askew;

And turn it towards hope, love, faith and peace,

And you will find in the end, an Eternal release.

THE WAR I REFUSE TO FIGHT
3/27/2018

It's becoming clearer every day; the that's war being fought,
Between brother, sister, man and wife; hearts are tuning to rot.
There's fighting, bickering, slandering and putting others down,
Yet in the end, can you find anyone actually wearing a crown?
Many find joy in stomping another's small fire out,
Can they not see the darkness they are creating all about?
Others try to force their views, like they are the only way.
Do we not live in a land of freedom for all to have their say?
What's the point in always putting the other guy down?
Do you really enjoy the strain of constantly wearing a frown?
Why do we hide our similarities and only bring differences up?
In the end must we not all drink from the same bitter cup?
Do you think the riches of this world are all you can achieve?
Do you think the glory of beating someone can change the way they believe?
Why do we continue the cycle of hurting others when we've been hurt,
Why when we have fallen, do we knock others into the dirt?
Have you never had a time in your life, another has offered a hand?
Have you never slowed down at all to hear nature's wonderful band?
Conversations and debates are healthy, to help you think for yourself,
Yet putting someone down for their beliefs, will not improve your wealth.
The evil one will always fight, he will never have quite enough,
If you let him control your heart, your road will always be rough.
When you push others away, putting more baggage on your back,
You really make it easier to fall again, while walking on your track.

We'll need each other in the end when we see the bigger picture,
For we all have different strengths and gifts, we must add to the mixture.
So, I will not engage to blaspheme or fight people anymore,
Unless, by chance, a fight is brought upon my very door.
Then I'll protect family and friends, feeling love still for my enemy,
Because tomorrow, they may humble themselves to ask for help from me.
I have been in pain before, and couldn't see beyond the lies,
And others were waiting patiently to comfort all my cries.

So today I wait patiently, for others who may need a friend,
For I finally see we are all brothers and sisters in the end.
There's a life worth so much more than fighting each other will attain;
A life of love and harmony, in which we can forever remain.
The enemy is not one of flesh or blood or bone,
It is the negativity inside that hides our light when it is shown.
That's why we must lift each other in times of need or hurt,
And stop letting the evil one win, by arguing things of no worth.
Look in a child's eyes, before he's been corrupted,
Before the lies of differences, his love had interrupted.
Those are the very eyes, where truth can really be found,
Of the Creator from above, who made us from the ground.
He sent us here to test us, so we could overcome,
The pride that this world creates in us and learn to become as one.
We cannot make it on our own, this has been proved by all,
From the very beginning when Adam had his first fall.
God then sent children to help him get back to a life of respect,
For he had to work for his freedom, and others he had to protect.
God never did let Adam, abide this life alone,
He knew love burned brighter, if to others it is shown.
So please if you are struggling, don't lash out on one another,
Instead see how you can help and lift a fellow brother.
Tomorrow it may be you, who needs a comforting smile,
So why don't we offer another a compliment, once in a while.
Instead of attacking others and making them feel small,
Let us stand united, against negativity, once and for all.

THE MIGHTY FOE 3/22/2018

There's a poem I once wrote about a mighty foe,
It's like a dream when I think of so long ago.
Back then it was just an average name,
Of a liquid substance some drank in shame.
I knew it caused problems it was easy to see,
I couldn't fathom to drink it, in the naive little me.
No one could make me, of that I was sure,
My heart was still open, my intentions were pure.
When I had been offered my first little drink,
Something inside me decided not to shrink.
I took a sip that I liked, then guzzled it down.
If I had anymore I knew I would drown.
So I swore I would never pick it up again;
Then my heart got shattered and my story began:
Alcohol started to be my best friend.
Anytime I was heartbroken it had an ear to lend.
Every time I was scared it gave me a hand,
To help fight my battles or bury me in sand.
When I was cold it warmed me right up.
If I was tired it was a great pick-me-up.
I was lonely a lot, and it made me new friends,
However, it blinded me to all the dead ends.
When at last I was shown the life I was leading,
It was like a horror book I was reading.
I had pushed away the ones I loved most.
The face in the mirror, was but a scared little ghost.
The light in my eyes had completely diminished,
And I knew at that moment, I had to be finished.

I had hurt many people and blamed it on them;
Really I was hurting myself, over and over again.
I've thought many times of the damage I've done,
Now with God's help, I know that I've won.
The binds of this monster are finally falling off,
Though I feel it inside and hear it scoff.
It says I can't do it, that I'll never win.
It says I'm not worthy, that I should give in.
When I refuse to let the fight go on,
I give it to God, that these fears may be gone.
I know that He'll help me, He's given me tools,
To help me swim across the negativity pools.
Some days it's harder to escape the madness;
Those days I am grateful, not full of sadness.
For those days remind me how far I have traveled,
And show me that alcohol's binds have unraveled.
Now instead of running or hiding somewhere,
I know I can turn to someone who'll share,
Their experience, love, understanding and peace.
There are plenty of others who have found release.
I know I can turn to God, church or family,
Or if I'm not ready I have friends who will hear me.
Some strangers are willing to listen, I'm learning,
For their past has also left their heart burning.
So try as you may, you will never win,
For mighty foe named Alcohol, I will not let you in.
My heart now, does not have the space;
It is a grateful, loving, and peaceful place.
And as long as I listen, and let God run the show,
He will tie my life together, not with binds; with a bow.

A NEW START 12/26/2018

Gratitude is something, I try to live each day,

It's more than just a thank you, while passing on my way.

It's a lifestyle I have learned, that helps me overcome,

The struggles I am going through, and the battles I have won.

It's a pathway to a freedom, money can't attain,

Where fear of loss and heartbreak, no longer can remain.

Many things have happened, in my crazy life.

The pain from some of them, still cut me like a knife.

Though I know that these memories, still make me sad some days,

I know the pain is fading, into a blurry haze.

I have hope in my heart, and faith in my spirit,

For now, I can help others, as they go through it.

There are many God dots, I'm seeing each day,

And I'm learning to connect them, no matter where they lay.

I cannot change my past, or predict the future,

I only have today, for healing to occur.

Many opportunities, for choices I can make,

Are laying right in front of me, my faith I won't forsake.

Joy fills my being, when after a rough day,

I have not gone backwards, and the old me is at bay.

This journey is exciting, when lessons I have learned,

And the bridges get rebuilt, that in my past I burned.

I now have a chance, at slowly finally living,

The life that I've been dreaming of; the chances God keeps giving.

I know I'll make mistakes, and sometimes I'll be selfish,

Some fires I will start, that I cannot extinguish.

I have hope with help from others, and a loving Father,

That I can make amends, become a better author.

The story I want told, when I leave this earth,

Is I did my best; to show others they have worth.

I'm grateful in my heart, each night I go to bed,

For I'm living a new life, not knowing what's ahead.

And each day that I wonder, if I'm all alone,

I now have a foundation, not made with sand, but stone.

SISTER OF THE NIGHT 06/14/2018

I look at the Moon and wonder, as she shines so very bright,
That even through all she's suffered, she shows up day and night.
She doesn't care that comets, have hit her many times,
She doesn't care that Earth, can hide the Sun that shines.
She doesn't mind the vastness, the universe entails,
She just moves around so gracefully, as if guided by handrails.
She glides above the storms, while we all run and hide,
She's not restricted by the laws, that we create and 'must' abide.
Money is just an object, no value to her at all,
She knows the only value, that matters is her call.
She doesn't dress to impress, like most are prone to do,
She shows up as herself, as God intended her to.
She stays above the surface, and gently guides below,
To help the ships being tossed, by the winds that blow.
She spreads her light to all in need, who may have lost their way,
She is not phased by negativity, no matter what we say.
She does her best to block, the rest of us down here,
From many hurdling objects, that may cause us to fear.
When perhaps it seems she fails, and something passes by,
She does not hide in shame or focuses on why.
She simply continues onward, following the plan,
There are others she must help; she does the best she can.

We all can learn a lot, from our sister of the night,
About the way to do our duty, to show another light.
It means to be ourselves, no matter what may come,
Remembering our workload, is an individual one.
We must keep moving forward, even showered by some pain,
Though it's not that easy, we have muscles to attain.
It seems we are not perfect, as the world may choose to view,
However, we have power, and each day we start anew.
We must love all those around us, and help them as we're able,
Especially if their rations, are barer at the table.
By doing our simple duty, of showing love to others,
We can help them move forward, our sisters and our brothers.
They too have a duty, that only they can know,
To help someone else, out of the winds that blow.
We cannot know another's future, ours are even blurred,
We cannot judge them by, past mistakes that have occurred.
Our paths will cross many times, and though we may not see,
They may have blocked a path or two, that we weren't meant to be.
So, as we go about our lives, I hope we can remember,
To do the very best we can, January to December.
One day we'll see God's grand design, and all the ways we meshed,
If we gave light to just one person, we'll know we did our best.

SISTER GAIA/MOTHER EARTH

11/22/2017

She lives, she breathes, she moves with a quiver,

Though you may never see her heart, lungs or liver.

She laughs, she rejoices, and sometimes she cries,

She knows our presence here though we can't see her eyes.

She speaks and she yells, with a thunderous clap,

And sometimes she whispers in the wind at our back.

She gives us the things we need to survive.

So why can't we admit she's even alive?

Water, food, shelter, warmth from above;

She even surrounds us with energy and love.

We cut, burn and dig to try to control her,

Yet we rarely turn around and remember to thank her.

I am just as guilty as anyone else,

So, I'm trying to change how I treat her myself.

Instead of giving her any type of abuse,

I really am trying to be of better use.

I try not to pick flowers or leaves anymore,

Because they are connected through the roots in the floor.

If there is an animal in pain or in need,

I try to help out, to comfort or feed.

We don't have to hug trees to show her we care,

Just picking up trash can help clean the air.

We may never be perfect and that's alright,

We just have to respect her so she keeps up the fight.

RED BIRD 02/15/2018

I wonder what the red bird sings as he's sitting on the branch,
Would the words of his song create a mighty avalanche?
I wonder what his lyrics mean that I have yet to understand,
If I sing his words to you, would it mean the same without a band?
I wonder if his thoughts would be of fear like most of us,
Or would they be so powerful that my brain would turn to dust?
I wonder how his day unveils, does he worry like we do,
Or does he just fly around knowing God will guide him through?
I wonder if the day will come, I can sit down by his side,
And learn how I can keep my song with me through the ride.
I wonder if he truly knows the love I feel for him,
For just like every creation of God, I see him as my kin.

Internal Struggle

THE WOLVES 02/03/2025

One wolf, inside, is getting strong, by feeding on the light;
The other one, who seeks the dark, in blindness, tries to bite.
I used to thrive in darkness, seeking to be numb;
They say the one we feed, will tend to overcome.
I stopped feeding Darkness, when I saw his lies;
He was getting even stronger, eating my insides.
Taking liberties to weaken me so I couldn't fight;
Now, the other wolf, duplicates the light.
Since I've been feeding Light, I finally feel at ease;
Yet I still feel Darkness, his breath is like a breeze.
When Light fills every crevice, I feel my muscles building;
I'll never really know, all the things he's shielding.
As I'm taking in more light, I know I'm getting stronger;
My list of reasons to continue, is slowly getting longer.
The wolf of light shines brighter, when the dark one goes to sleep;
I must maintain good habits, to support upkeep.
Though he may lie dormant, Darkness hasn't retreated;
One day I'll meet the Source of Light, then Dark will be defeated.
Until that day arrives, whenever he has stirred;
I hope I put more light inside, Dark's eyesight to be blurred.
Darkness cannot win, when feeding the wolf of light;
I know that in the end, it will be worth the fight.

MY REALITY 7/09/2017

In an alternate reality, of days long past,

Stood a broken little girl, in a rock hard cast.

No one really loved her, that was what she thought.

In her mind she was abandoned, left alone to rot.

People all around her, would pick on her or tease,

Taking it all personal, she told her heart to freeze.

Her pain grew even deeper, when someone took advantage;

So she knew she had to run, her emotions she must manage.

The beginning was to fake a smile, in every situation;

Becoming a chameleon, so she could prove her station.

Next were the addictions, manipulating, lying;

Before she even realized it, no longer was she trying.

It became a way of life, no effort left at all;

To run or drink her life away, was her only call.

Going through the motions, not letting others in,

She felt that to pretend, was the only way to win.

She saw glimmers here and there, never finding peace,

Running to wrong places, to try to get release.

The people she kept close, she loved as best she could.

Most were lost just like her, clinging to falsehood.

The ruin this was causing, never crossed her mind;

Her worth she had been walking on, so hope was hard to find.

It took her long to realize, her perspectives were all wrong;

She was worthy of true love; she had been all along.

With this simple knowledge, lines were surely shifted,
The weights of old realities were slowly being lifted.
The past provided lessons, for healing to occur.
She learned to focus on today, for the future was a blur.
Now in this strange new realm, unfolding every day,
Stands a hopeful little girl, discovering her way.
Vulnerable and open, to learn humility;
Willing to make progress, towards the day she's free;
She fights a daily battle, forgiveness to attain,
For from her past reality, resentments do remain.
She has to snuff the urges, of building up more walls;
Especially when she feels, she's had too many falls.
She only knows the next right step, is opening her heart,
To that Holy Power; He'll outline her part.
He's watched her all along, providing her protection,
She no longer tries, to run from that connection.
She does not thrive in chaos or causing a commotion.
She can stand her ground, not hiding from emotion.
The unknown, though a mystery, no longer is so scary,
If the present is unpleasant, she knows it's temporary.
She gets up if she falls and holds her head up high.
She knows that it's okay, if she needs to cry.
Continuing this daily, her past no longer binds,
And on anxieties of tomorrow, she can lower blinds.
Not knowing what the future brings, is but a tiny cost,
The blessing of uncertainty? She is no longer lost.

SHE IS ME 01/23/2025

I am still afraid of me, at least the me I used to be.

I want to love her and forgive, I feel I must so I can live.

Looking at my past mistakes, I am reliving past heartaches.

I hurt others and myself; my heart was hidden on a shelf.

Aggressor, victim; both within, intertwined around the sin.

Drinking, drugging, people too; any high I would pursue.

Resentment, aplenty, on my mind, held me tight like chains that bind.

The hurt in others I could see; I often used them to help me.

I wouldn't admit when I had betrayed, I couldn't look back at scars I made.

I just blamed them for their flaws; as I look back, I have to pause.

I see the patterns I have sewn, the damage caused has been shown.

With some hindsight I have borrowed, I'm changing roads I have followed.

God is showing me new ways, to escape resentment's maze.

I'm learning how to make amends, seeking to reset the trends.

I'm learning love for old me, one day maybe I can see,

She wasn't bad, she was sick; being afraid is a mind trick.

I do not need to hold fear; she's been healed by the One who's near.

She is not some distant monster, she is me, I already love her.

Sharing the Message of Light

PAYING IT FORWARD 04/08/2018

I'm not sure what to write about, yet I know that this is right.
I have to keep using my words to stay within the fight.
The fight for freedom and happiness has to begin with me;
Or else my world is doomed, for all eternity.
God gave me a voice to speak, in speaking I can find,
The strength to move forward, if only in my mind.
Writing helps release, the bonds upon my heart,
I know I'll never be finished; this is just a start.
The journey is a long one, I know without a doubt.
Sometimes I want to cry, others I need to shout.
That does not diminish, the power of my words,
For sometimes they take flight, just like little birds;
To a broken heart that needs hope and love within,
So, on their own long journey, they can finally begin.
There are many in this world suffering as I did,
Because they felt alone, like a lost little kid.
Someone was always there, though to them I was blind,
And as I look within my past, it's not that hard to find;
That though I felt alone, someone was always there,
To help me lift my load, my burden they did share.
Maybe it was church, or family or a friend,
Mostly it was strangers, who had a hand to lend.
Whether it was a smile, or a kind word when required,
Even though I couldn't see, hope never retired.
I'd see the love of a child, who shyly waved a hand,
Or saw a smile on someone, who heard their favorite band.
I have seen many men, who hold open many doors,
And when I have dropped something, some got on all fours,

To help me gather up, my items on the ground,
And even if I didn't thank them, malice wasn't found.
There truly are kind people, who genuinely care,
Even if my love inside, is feeling very bare.
I ask for God instead, to let me be His light,
I know that He protects me, so I thank Him every night.
He shows me how I can help, another in distress,
Sometimes I don't know how, this I must confess.
So, I have to open my mouth and ask for what they need.
Even if they say nothing, I know I kept my creed,
The one I made to God, that I love my fellow brother,
And if they are not ready for help, I turn to another.
If only to plant a seed, from God who knows the best,
For others He will send, to take care of the rest.
We all need each other, to fill our hearts with memories,
So, we can see God moments, that show up in our stories.
I hope one day I see, everyone involved,
That helped me on my way, while this world revolved.
I know I wouldn't make it, traveling alone,
I'm glad that there were others whose light I was shone.
Though fear, anger, sadness, still remain inside,
I'm not worried any more, for love now does reside.
Inside where there were cobwebs, God shook them from the wall,
So, off the cliff of negativity, I didn't have to fall.
Now I must repay, the kindness that He gave me,
By sending other people, in my life to save me.
I will try forever more, to help others every day,
To give someone light, to help them on their way.
I know if I can do this, God won't let me down,
Because when I am lost, to Him I'm always found.

JUST WRITE 01/13/2025

I write because it sets me free; I write so others can see me.

When pen hits paper, all is well; it's like I'm under quite a spell.

It comes to me in bits and pieces; I find the words in the paper's creases.

Sometimes I type them on a screen, the medium doesn't matter to set the scene.

Getting the message out of my mind, helps to loosen the chains that bind.

The ones that try to strangle my voice, telling me I have no choice.

That I must keep faith to myself, my words should never leave the shelf.

They tell me that my message is false, sometimes I get sick of dancing this waltz.

It's all just lies to crush my spirit, to keep me small; I won't hear it.

My voice was given by the One, who sent to Earth, His holy Son.

When I listen with my heart, the words He slowly does impart.

Often, I write of fear and pain and show that hope does still remain.

Writing gives me joy and peace; it's given me a great release;

A place to share the deepest things, that bind my mind as if with strings.

A place for faith and dreams to bare, so others may see, and find strength to share;

Their pain and love, faith and fears; to also help others throughout the years.

My hope is, one day, by using my voice, I may help others to have the choice;

To find their own, so they can be free, and feel God's love, just like me.

If I get stuck, the words hard to find, I search the corners of my mind.

I find new words that mean the same, original messages sometimes remain.

Many times, however, if my heart is open; God changes things, His message to be spoken.

I know I'm not perfect at sharing His light, yet I tell myself often, "Don't fear, just write."

God opens the hearts of those who read, my words are often just a seed;

A way for others to see His hand, how He has helped me heal and stand,

After all my many falls and show how He broke my many walls,

The ones I built to keep others out. Now as I move forward, I will gladly shout,

About the hope I get from above, and the warmth of Heavenly Love.

One day God will stop the internal fight; until then, I'll continue to just write.

PHOTOS

ABOUT THE AUTHOR

MARIE SLIDER HENRIKSEN has been creative since childhood and writing since she was a teenager. Years ago, when she got sober, her love of writing was rejuvenated. While in recovery from alcoholism, drugs, food addiction, and PTSD, she pursued a journey of healing and spirituality. Marie is also recovering from a lesser-known condition, Ehlers Danlos Syndrome (EDS), which is caused by a mutation in a specific gene, affecting the connective tissue in her body.

Marie grew up in Mesa, Arizona, but lived many places before, during, and after her service in the United States Army. She has an AA in General Education, is close to receiving her AS in Family History, and her BS in Professional Studies.

Marie is active in her community doing her best to support others in their recovery and spirituality. She especially seeks to bring awareness of veteran suicide and to encourage other veterans to seek healing. When her energy allows, she loves to be in nature, walking or driving, and feels it is the best way for her to get close to God. Music has also been a huge factor in her healing journey; whether listening, singing, or writing her own songs. She currently resides in Kaysville, Utah with her husband, and is a member of The Church of Jesus Christ of Latter-Day Saints.

Marie encourages everyone, to write, at least to journal. She hopes that as you shake off your own chains of fear, resentment, and addictions, you can also one day say to yourself as she has, "I am More Me Than I Used to Be."

CONTACT THE AUTHOR

Marie Slider Henriksen

Recovery Advocate • Author • Podcaster

See my work and contact me:

Website: **sliderbabe.com** • Email: marie@sliderbabe.com

Please join **Sliderbabe on Facebook**,
to Creatively Heal Out Loud Through Community.

Ask me about a non-profit partnership for donating books to facilities, to promote healing and recovery.

www.ingramcontent.com/pod-product-compliance
Lightning Source LLC
Chambersburg PA
CBHW041518120626
46551CB00018B/2474